Professionalizing the Nation's Cybersecurity Workforce?

Criteria for Decision-Making

Committee on Professionalizing the Nation's Cybersecurity Workforce:
Criteria for Future Decision-Making

Computer Science and Telecommunications Board

Division on Engineering and Physical Sciences

NATIONAL RESEARCH COUNCIL
OF THE NATIONAL ACADEMIES

THE NATIONAL ACADEMIES PRESS
Washington, D.C.
www.nap.edu

THE NATIONAL ACADEMIES PRESS   500 Fifth Street, NW   Washington, DC 20001

NOTICE: The project that is the subject of this report was approved by the Governing Board of the National Research Council, whose members are drawn from the councils of the National Academy of Sciences, the National Academy of Engineering, and the Institute of Medicine. The members of the committee responsible for the report were chosen for their special competences and with regard for appropriate balance.

This project was supported by the U.S. Department of Homeland Security under Contract No. HSHQDC-11-D-00009, Task Order No. HSHQDC-12-J-00157. Any opinions, findings, conclusions, or recommendations expressed in this publication are those of the author(s) and do not necessarily reflect the view of the organizations or agencies that provided support for this project.

International Standard Book Number-13:   978-0-309-29104-0
International Standard Book Number-10:   0-309-29104-6

Additional copies of this workshop summary are available for sale from the National Academies Press, 500 Fifth Street, NW, Keck 360, Washington, DC 20001; (800) 624-6242 or (202) 334-3313; http://www.nap.edu.

Copyright 2013 by the National Academy of Sciences. All rights reserved.

Printed in the United States of America

THE NATIONAL ACADEMIES
Advisers to the Nation on Science, Engineering, and Medicine

The **National Academy of Sciences** is a private, nonprofit, self-perpetuating society of distinguished scholars engaged in scientific and engineering research, dedicated to the furtherance of science and technology and to their use for the general welfare. Upon the authority of the charter granted to it by the Congress in 1863, the Academy has a mandate that requires it to advise the federal government on scientific and technical matters. Dr. Ralph J. Cicerone is president of the National Academy of Sciences.

The **National Academy of Engineering** was established in 1964, under the charter of the National Academy of Sciences, as a parallel organization of outstanding engineers. It is autonomous in its administration and in the selection of its members, sharing with the National Academy of Sciences the responsibility for advising the federal government. The National Academy of Engineering also sponsors engineering programs aimed at meeting national needs, encourages education and research, and recognizes the superior achievements of engineers. Dr. C. D. Mote, Jr., is president of the National Academy of Engineering.

The **Institute of Medicine** was established in 1970 by the National Academy of Sciences to secure the services of eminent members of appropriate professions in the examination of policy matters pertaining to the health of the public. The Institute acts under the responsibility given to the National Academy of Sciences by its congressional charter to be an adviser to the federal government and, upon its own initiative, to identify issues of medical care, research, and education. Dr. Harvey V. Fineberg is president of the Institute of Medicine.

The **National Research Council** was organized by the National Academy of Sciences in 1916 to associate the broad community of science and technology with the Academy's purposes of furthering knowledge and advising the federal government. Functioning in accordance with general policies determined by the Academy, the Council has become the principal operating agency of both the National Academy of Sciences and the National Academy of Engineering in providing services to the government, the public, and the scientific and engineering communities. The Council is administered jointly by both Academies and the Institute of Medicine. Dr. Ralph J. Cicerone and Dr. C. D. Mote, Jr., are chair and vice chair, respectively, of the National Research Council.

www.national-academies.org

**COMMITTEE ON PROFESSIONALIZING THE
NATION'S CYBERSECURITY WORKFORCE:
CRITERIA FOR FUTURE DECISION-MAKING**

DIANA L. BURLEY, George Washington University, *Co-Chair*
SEYMOUR E. GOODMAN, Georgia Institute of Technology, *Co-Chair*
MATT BISHOP, University of California, Davis
MISCHEL L. KWON, Mischel Kwon and Associates, LLC
KEVIN R. MURPHY, Colorado State University
PHILIP M. NECHES, Foundation Ventures, LLC.
CHARLES "CASEY" O'BRIEN, National CyberWatch Center,
    Prince George's Community College
RONALD P. SANDERS, Booz Allen Hamilton

Staff

JON EISENBERG, Director, Computer Science and Telecommunications
    Board
ENITA A. WILLIAMS, Associate Program Officer (through April 2013)
SHENAE BRADLEY, Senior Program Assistant

COMPUTER SCIENCE AND TELECOMMUNICATIONS BOARD

ROBERT F. SPROULL, Oracle (retired), *Chair*
LUIZ ANDRÉ BARROSO, Google, Inc.
ROBERT BRAMMER, Brammer Technology, LLC
EDWARD FRANK, Apple, Inc.
JACK L. GOLDSMITH III, Harvard Law School
SEYMOUR E. GOODMAN, Georgia Institute of Technology
LAURA M. HAAS, IBM Amalden Research Laboratory
ROBERT HOROWITZ, Stanford University
MICHAEL KEARNS, University of Pennsylvania
ROBERT KRAUT, Carnegie Mellon University
SUSAN LANDAU, Radcliffe Institute for Advanced Study
PETER LEE, Microsoft Corporation
DAVID E. LIDDLE, U.S. Venture Partners
BARBARA LISKOV, Massachusetts Institute of Technology
JOHN STANKOVIC, University of Virginia
JOHN A. SWAINSON, Dell, Inc.
PETER SZOLOVITS, Massachusetts Institute of Technology
ERNEST J. WILSON, University of Southern California
KATHERINE YELICK, University of California, Berkeley

Staff

JON EISENBERG, Director
VIRGINIA BACON TALATI, Program Officer
SHENAE BRADLEY, Senior Program Assistant
RENEE HAWKINS, Financial and Administrative Manager
HERBERT S. LIN, Chief Scientist
LYNETTE I. MILLETT, Associate Director
ERIC WHITAKER, Senior Program Assistant

For more information on CSTB, see its website at
http://www.cstb.org; write to CSTB, National Research Council,
500 Fifth Street, NW, Washington, DC 20001; call (202) 334-2605; or
e-mail CSTB at cstb@nas.edu.

Preface

The federal National Initiative for Cybersecurity Education (NICE) aims to "enhance the overall cybersecurity posture of the United States by accelerating the availability of educational and training resources designed to improve the cyber behavior, skills, and knowledge of every segment of the population."[1] One of the issues being considered as part of NICE is the role of professionalization in enhancing the cybersecurity workforce. The U.S. Department of Homeland Security (DHS), one of the agencies carrying out activities under NICE, lists three questions regarding the role of professionalization on the National Initiative for Cybersecurity Careers and Studies webpage on cybersecurity professionalization:

- Is cybersecurity ready to be professionalized across the nation?
- Which jobs within the cybersecurity field should be professionalized and to what degree?
- Should the federal government lead this effort single handedly?[2]

That page goes on to describe the present study, sponsored by DHS, on professionalization. Box P.1 provides the full statement of task. To carry out the study, the Committee on Professionalizing the Nation's Cyber-

---

[1] U.S. Department of Homeland Security, National Initiative for Cybersecurity Careers and Studies (NICCS), About the National Initiative for Cybersecurity Education, available at http://niccs.us-cert.gov/footer/about-nice.

[2] U.S. Department of Homeland Security, National Initiative for Cybersecurity Careers and Studies, Professionalization, available at http://niccs.us-cert.gov/careers/professionalization.

> **BOX P.1**
> **Statement of Task**
>
> An ad hoc committee will conduct a study that would consider approaches to increasing the professionalization of the nation's cybersecurity workforce. It would examine workforce requirements for cybersecurity and the segments and job functions in which professionalization is most needed; the role of assessment tools, certification, licensing, and other means for assessing and enhancing professionalization; and emerging approaches, such as performance-based measures. It would also examine requirements for the federal (military and civilian) workforce, the private sector, and state and local government.
>
> Three public workshops would be held in the course of the study as the principal data-gathering events to obtain input on the foregoing issues from education and training institutions and public and private sector employers of cybersecurity workers. The committee will develop the respective agendas, select and invite speakers and discussants, and moderate the discussions. Subsequently, the committee will prepare a report, drawing on the workshops. The report would characterize the current landscape for cybersecurity workforce development and set forth criteria that the federal agencies participating in the National Initiative for Cybersecurity Education—as well as organizations that employ cybersecurity workers—could use to identify which specialty areas may require professionalization and to evaluate different approaches and tools for professionalization.

security Workforce: Criteria for Future Decision-Making was convened under the auspices of the Computer Science and Telecommunications Board of the National Research Council (Appendix A).

The statement of task speaks broadly about a range of matters to be considered or examined. With one exception noted below, the committee did explore all of these points. Consistent with discussions with DHS before and during the study as well as with the time and resources available for the study, the committee took as its central task to do what is called for in the final sentence of the statement of task—to prepare a report that would

> Characterize the current landscape for cybersecurity workforce development and set forth criteria that the federal agencies participating in the National Initiative for Cybersecurity Education—as well as organizations that employ cybersecurity workers—could use to identify which specialty areas may require professionalization and to evaluate different approaches and tools for professionalization.

In developing this report, the committee identified three essential elements—(1) understanding the context for cybersecurity workforce development; (2) considering the relative advantages, disadvantages, and approaches to professionalizing the nation's cybersecurity workforce; and (3) setting forth criteria that can be used to identify which, if any, specialty areas may require professionalization—and set forth criteria for evaluating different approaches and tools for professionalization. As called for in the statement of task, the committee considered these in the context of the national cybersecurity workforce—and, in particular, not just with respect to the federal government workforce. One issue that is listed in the statement of task but is not addressed in this report is the question of approaches to performance assessment. The reason for this omission is simple: the committee did not hear about this point at the workshops it convened. The committee believes that this issue will merit more attention in the future as professionalization measures are implemented and refined.

The principal input to this study came from a series of three workshops convened by the study committee and held in Washington, D.C., San Francisco, California (coinciding with and partly co-located with the RSA Conference), and San Antonio, Texas. An additional data-gathering meeting with approximately 25 attendees was held at the Cybercorps Scholarship for Service principal investigators' meeting on January 10, 2013, in Arlington, Virginia. Agendas for the three workshops organized by the committee are provided in Appendix B. Speakers at the workshops came from organizations associated with the education and development of cybersecurity workers (community colleges, colleges, and universities; organizations that provide certificates and certifications, and professional associations); organizations that employ cybersecurity workers (federal, state, and local government and a wide array of private sector firms). Speakers also included students and a diverse set of people who hold cybersecurity jobs or whose positions significantly involve cybersecurity. Within the federal government, speakers came from civilian, law enforcement, defense, and intelligence agencies. Speakers from private firms included individuals from the information technology, cybersecurity, entertainment, banking and finance, and manufacturing sectors. Lists of speakers and participants in the three workshops are provided in Appendix C. A principal focus of the workshops and other interactions was to understand how organizations think about cybersecurity jobs and the role of professionalization. In the course of these presentations and discussions, the committee heard almost every imaginable point of view, and many points were both corroborated and contradicted by other speakers.

During the course of the study, the committee also reviewed reports related to the cybersecurity workforce in general and to its professionalization in particular. These reports provide a variety of perspectives on the need, demand, and supply for cybersecurity workers, the sorts of skills required, and ways of improving the capacity and capability of the workforce. Some of these reports focused on the federal government workforce, while others looked at the workforce more broadly. Some are independent analysis, and others were prepared by groups with a particular interest in some aspect of workforce issues.

Chapters 1 and 2 provide context regarding the cybersecurity challenge, the role of the cybersecurity workforce in addressing this challenge, and the role that professionalization might play. Chapter 3 provides the committee's analysis and its conclusions and recommendation.

We would like to thank the Department of Homeland Security for sponsoring this study and acknowledge in particular the assistance of Robin "Montana" Williams, branch chief, Cybersecurity Education and Awareness, U.S. Department of Homeland Security. We would also like to acknowledge the contributions made by the speakers and participants at the three workshops organized by the committee.

> Diana Burley and Seymour Goodman, *Co-Chairs*
> Committee on Professionalizing the
> Nation's Cybersecurity Workforce:
> Criteria for Future Decision-Making

Acknowledgment of Reviewers

This report has been reviewed in draft form by individuals chosen for their diverse perspectives and technical expertise, in accordance with procedures approved by the National Research Council's Report Review Committee. The purpose of this independent review is to provide candid and critical comments that will assist the institution in making its published report as sound as possible and to ensure that the report meets institutional standards for objectivity, evidence, and responsiveness to the study charge. The review comments and draft manuscript remain confidential to protect the integrity of the deliberative process. We wish to thank the following individuals for their review of this report:

Byron Collie, Goldman Sachs Group, Inc.,
Stephen Cooper, Stanford University,
Paul E. Gray, Massachusetts Institute of Technology,
Cynthia Irvine, Naval Postgraduate School,
John D. Johnson, Deere & Company,
Anita Jones, University of Virginia,
Susan Landau, privacyink.org,
Fred Oswald, Rice University,
Michael Papay, Northrup Grumman Corporation,
Franklin S. Reeder, Reeder Group, Inc., and
Eugene Spafford, Purdue University.

Although the reviewers listed above have provided many constructive comments and suggestions, they were not asked to endorse the conclusions or recommendations, nor did they see the final draft of the report before its release. The review of this report was overseen by R. Stephen Berry, University of Chicago (emeritus). Appointed by the National Research Council, he was responsible for making certain that an independent examination of this report was carried out in accordance with institutional procedures and that all review comments were carefully considered. Responsibility for the final content of this report rests entirely with the authoring committee and the institution.

Contents

EXECUTIVE SUMMARY   1

1   CYBERSECURITY, THE CYBERSECURITY WORKFORCE,   5
AND ITS DEVELOPMENT AND PROFESSIONALIZATION
Cybersecurity, 5
Need, Demand, and Supply, 7
Roles, Responsibilities, and Contexts for Cybersecurity Work, 9
Factors Affecting Future Cybersecurity Workforce Needs, 12

2   APPROACHES TO PROFESSIONALIZATION   14
Profession, 14
Professionalization, 15
Goals for Professionalization, 16
Specific Mechanisms for Professionalization and How They
   Affect Workforce Capacity and Capability, 17
Timescales for Professionalization, 20
Trade-offs Associated with Professionalization, 20

3   CONCLUSIONS, RECOMMENDATION, AND CRITERIA   23
FOR PROFESSIONALIZATION OF CYBERSECURITY
Capacity and Capability of the Cybersecurity Workforce, 23
Cybersecurity Work and the Cybersecurity Workforce, 24
Professionalization, 26
Criteria, 28

APPENDIXES

A	Biographies of Committee Members	33
B	Workshop Agendas	39
C	Speakers and Participants at Workshops Organized by the Committee	47

Executive Summary

The nation's cybersecurity challenge stems from threats from a wide array of actors who seek to compromise the confidentiality, integrity, and availability of elements of cyberspace by exploiting flaws in the design, implementation, configuration, and operation of information technology systems. This cybersecurity threat faces individuals, organizations of all sizes, and government at all levels.

The effort to establish a safer and more secure cyberspace will require improvements in many areas, including a cybersecurity workforce that has the capacity and capability to do the job; better tools and techniques that enhance the efficiency and effectiveness of cybersecurity workers; better tools and approaches for risk identification and assessment; better systems design and development; greater incentives to encourage the deployment of better cybersecurity technologies and practices; improvements in end-user behavior through training; and organizational, national, and international measures to deter bad actors.

This report considers the role that professionalization might play in ensuring that the United States has a cybersecurity workforce with enough cybersecurity workers (capacity) with the right knowledge, skills, and abilities (capability). The committee understood its principal tasks to be (1) to consider the role that professionalization could play in enhancing the capacity and capability of the national cybersecurity workforce and (2) to identify criteria that could be used by decision-makers in government and the private sector when considering measures to professionalize the cybersecurity workforce.

In brief, the committee found that although the occupations comprising the field of cybersecurity do require specialized knowledge and some form of intensive advanced training, they have not yet sufficiently crystallized into specific professions. Cybersecurity is a young field, and the technologies, threats, and actions taken to counter the threats that characterize the endeavor are changing too rapidly to risk imposing the rigidities that typically attend professional status. Some organizations may find that professionalization provides a useful degree of "quality control" for those who work in the field, but professionalization also imposes barriers to those who wish to enter the field at a time when demand for cybersecurity workers exceeds supply.

CAPACITY AND CAPABILITY OF THE CYBERSECURITY WORKFORCE

Conclusion 1. More attention to both the capacity and capability of the U.S. cybersecurity workforce is needed.

Conclusion 2. Although the need for cybersecurity workers is likely to continue to be high, it is difficult to forecast with certainty the number of workers required or the needed mix of cybersecurity knowledge and skills.

CYBERSECURITY WORK AND THE CYBERSECURITY WORKFORCE

Conclusion 3. The cybersecurity workforce encompasses a variety of contexts, roles, and occupations and is too broad and diverse to be treated as a single occupation or profession. Whether and how to professionalize will vary according to role and context.

Conclusion 4. Because cybersecurity is not solely a technical endeavor, a wide range of backgrounds and skills will be needed in an effective national cybersecurity workforce.

PROFESSIONALIZATION

Conclusion 5. Professionalization has multiple goals and can occur through multiple mechanisms.

Conclusion 6. The path toward professionalization of a field can be slow and difficult, and not all portions of a field can or should be professionalized at the same time.

CRITERIA FOR DECISION-MAKING ABOUT PROFESSIONALIZATION

Conclusion 7. Professionalization has associated costs and benefits that should be weighed when making decisions to undertake professionalization activities.

Professionalization is not a proxy for "better," but it may be a useful tool in certain circumstances. The following criteria are suggested to help identify cybersecurity specialties and circumstances where professionalization may be appropriate and to assess the potential effects of different professionalization mechanisms:

- *Do the benefits of a given professionalization measure outweigh the potential supply restrictions resulting from the additional barriers to entry?*
- *Does the potential to provide additional information about a candidate outweigh the risks of false certainty about who is actually best suited for a job?*
- *Do the benefits of establishing the standards needed for professionalization outweigh the risks of obsolescence (when the knowledge or skills associated with the standard are out-of-date by the time a standard is agreed on) and ossification (when the establishment of a standard inhibits further development by workers of their skills and knowledge)?*

Recommendation. Activities by the federal government and other entities to professionalize a cybersecurity occupation should be undertaken only when that occupation has well-defined and stable characteristics, when there are observed deficiencies in the occupational workforce that professionalization could help remedy, and when the benefits outweigh the costs.

Cybersecurity is a broad field, and professionalization is something that can be undertaken for specific occupations within the field and not the field as a whole. Before professionalization activities are undertaken for an occupation, two high-level criteria should be met:

1. *The occupation has well-defined characteristics.* These include stable knowledge and skill requirements, stable roles and responsibilities and occupational boundaries that distinguish the profession from others, well-defined career ladders that provide links to professionalization mechanisms, and agreed-on ethical standards to which members of the profession will be held.
2. *There is credible evidence of deficiencies in the occupational workforce,* such as skill deficiencies, questions of legitimacy among the current set of practitioners, or concerns about accountability.

The criteria in Conclusion 7 speak to the trade-offs that should be considered by those seeking to professionalize those who work in the field of cybersecurity—including the U.S. government, other U.S. public and private employers, educational institutions, certification bodies, and so forth.

These trade-offs illustrate the complex set of costs and benefits associated with professionalization. Some of the uncertainties may diminish over time, and long-term benefits may ultimately outweigh short-term costs. It may thus be an effective strategy to encourage, rather than require, the use of certain professionalization mechanisms so as to avoid overly restricting supply in the short term while still establishing a long-term path to enhancing quality.

Over time, parts of the cybersecurity field will likely reach the point where professionalization will be warranted. The criteria set forth under the Recommendation can be used by decision makers to judge when that time has come.

1

Cybersecurity, the Cybersecurity Workforce, and Its Development and Professionalization

CYBERSECURITY

Cyberspace comprises myriad interconnected computers, cyber-physical systems, and telecommunications networks—including the Internet and the systems attached to it—that have become integral to our economy, society, and national security. These include servers, routers, and other infrastructure; desktops, laptops, and mobile computing devices; and the many other devices that incorporate computing and networking functionality. Cybersecurity involves the articulation and enforcement of security policies for information and communications systems and the implementation of associated technical solutions, mechanisms, and programs. These policies protect various desirable attributes of a system—for example, confidentiality, possession or control, integrity, authenticity, availability, and utility.[1] Privacy is closely associated with security; for example, confidentiality is required to protect information from unwanted disclosure. Cybersecurity is also required for safety when misuse of information and communications systems has the potential to cause harm.

The nation's cybersecurity challenge stems from actions taken by a wide array of actors—including individuals, insiders, criminal organizations, transnational nonstate actors, and nation-states—to compromise computing and communications systems and the organizations

---

[1] This particular framework comes from D.B. Parker, *Fighting Computer Crime,* John Wiley & Sons, New York, N.Y., 1998.

that depend on these systems. Indeed, the whole field of cybersecurity would not exist without these adversaries.[2] This cybersecurity threat faces individuals, organizations of all sizes, and government at all levels. The overall sense is that the threat is evolving and growing.[3] Because attackers target organizations and individuals as well as machines and networks, protecting cyberspace also means ensuring that the components are securely operated, and thus cybersecurity involves human and behavioral factors.

Although many of the fundamental cybersecurity challenges have endured over time, the underlying information and communications technologies and their applications continue to change rapidly. For example, recent years have seen the rapid adoption of smart phones and tablets by consumers and employers and the associated phenomenon of "bring your own device," which has rapidly infused mobile devices into the workplace. Both developments have provided organizations with new capabilities that introduce at the same time new cybersecurity risks. Cybersecurity threats also continue to evolve as the interests of active human adversaries change, as their capabilities grow, and as the techniques they employ change. The response to the cybersecurity threat has also shifted from one that was entirely, or at least primarily, defensive in nature to one that also includes more active activities, even as defensive activities continue to dominate. In the national security arena, the United States has made public its plans to strengthen its offensive cyber operations capabilities and workforce.

Although the prevailing sense is that the state of the nation's cybersecurity is not getting better (and indeed many argue that it is getting worse), it is actually difficult to measure how "cyber secure" a system, organization, or nation may be.[4] Consider, for example, that the security of a system generally reflects not only how well that system was constructed, but also how it is configured, the organizational policies and practices that govern its operation, the degree to which organizational members follow these policies, and the capabilities and interests of potential adversaries.[5] Moreover, organizations have different definitions of security (i.e., different security policies), so a system that is "secure" for

---

[2] Although dependability and other trustworthiness issues would remain.

[3] See, e.g., National Research Council, *Toward a Safer and More Secure Cyberspace*, The National Academies Press, Washington, D.C., 2007. The following provides a similar assessment of the situation facing the federal government: see U.S. Government Accountability Office, *Cybersecurity: National Strategy, Roles, and Responsibilities Need to Be Better Defined and More Effectively Implemented*, GAO-13-187, Washington, D.C., February 2013.

[4] See, e.g., National Research Council, *Toward a Safer and More Secure Cyberspace*, 2007, pp. 2 and 133.

[5] National Research Council, *Toward a Safer and More Secure Cyberspace*, 2007, pp. 133-135.

one use or one organization may not be secure for other uses or organizations. All of this makes it challenging to accurately assess workforce requirements, make workforce investment decisions, or measure the contributions or performance of the cybersecurity workforce.

The effort to establish a safer and more secure cyberspace will require improvements in many areas, including a cybersecurity workforce that has the capacity and capability to do the job; better tools and techniques that enhance the efficiency and effectiveness of cybersecurity workers; better tools and approaches for risk identification and assessment; better systems design; better systems-development practices; greater incentives to encourage the deployment of better cybersecurity technologies and practices; better practices and techniques for dealing with the supply chain for components and services; improvements in end-user behavior through training; and organizational, industry, national, and international measures to deter bad actors. This report focuses on one of these areas: building a cybersecurity workforce with enough cybersecurity workers of the right types (capacity) with the right knowledge, skills, and abilities (capability) and the improvements that might come from professionalization.

NEED, DEMAND, AND SUPPLY

The size of the cybersecurity workforce is difficult to measure because it spans many job roles that often have different and overlapping titles in different organizations. The Bureau of Labor Statistics estimated employment at 72,670* in 2010 for the occupation "information security analysts,"[6] a category that does not encompass all cybersecurity workers. An indication of the scale of that workforce segment in the federal government was provided by the size of the target population for a recent workforce survey by the Department of Homeland Security (DHS) and the Federal Chief Information Officer Council that was sent to more than 200,000 federal civilian employees from 82 agencies.[7] Some sense of the total cybersecurity-related workforce, construed broadly, can be obtained by considering the number of organizations that must undertake some

---

*Editor's note: Following initial publication of this report, this number was updated to reflect 2010 BLS data for the category in question. See the primary reference given in footnote 6.

[6] Bureau of Labor Statistics, U.S. Department of Labor, Occupational Employment and Wage, May 2012: 15-1122 Information Security Analysts, available at http://www.bls.gov/oes/current/oes151122.htm.

[7] National Initiative for Cybersecurity Education, Department of Homeland Security and Federal CIO Council, *2012 Information Technology Workforce Assessment for Cybersecurity Summary Report*, Washington, D.C., 2013.

measures to protect their cybersecurity. There are, for example, roughly 6 million businesses with a payroll (and many more without)[8] and nearly 90,000 local governments and public school systems[9] in the United States. Not all necessarily have full-time cybersecurity workers, but all must have someone responsible for that organization's cybersecurity, at least to make decisions about which information technology and cybersecurity products and services to acquire.

In considering the role of professionalization in building a cybersecurity workforce with sufficient capacity and capability, it is useful to distinguish need, demand, and supply. *Need* is the number (and skill mix) of cybersecurity workers required to provide satisfactory cybersecurity (a judgment that will vary according to who makes the assessment). *Demand* is expressed by the desired capabilities stated in job descriptions, the number of such positions that are created and filled, and the salaries offered to those who have those abilities. Demand will fall short of national or societal need to the extent that cybersecurity is a public good—that is, organizations will invest to meet their own requirements but not necessarily to achieve society's desirable overall requirements. Demand can also fall short of an organization's own needs if (1) the organization lacks the required resources or (2) an organization underestimates the threats it faces and thus underinvests in meeting its own needs. *Supply* is the number of available qualified[10] workers willing to fill positions and is a function of the visibility and attractiveness of cybersecurity occupations, the availability of appropriate training and education, and (as in all fields) the overall labor market in which potential workers respond to salary and other signals about demand.

As discussed below, professionalization mechanisms can both stimulate supply, by making a field more attractive, and dampen supply, by creating barriers to entry. They can make it easier for employers to meet their needs, by making it easier to identify suitable candidates, but they can also inhibit the flexibility needed as job requirements change or where job responsibilities are necessarily broad and fluid.

It would be helpful in assessing the role and effects of professionalization to have a handle on the current supply of cybersecurity workers. Unfortunately, it is notoriously difficult to assess labor supply and demand to determine whether or not there is a shortage. For example, employers in a particular sector may complain that they cannot find enough quali-

---

[8] U.S. Census Bureau, Statistics about Business Size, 2007, available at http://www.census.gov/econ/smallbus.html.

[9] U.S. Census Bureau, Local Government and Public School Systems by Type and State, 2007, available at http://www.census.gov/govs/cog/GovOrgTab03ss.html.

[10] Without ways of assessing quality, the supply will, of course, include available but unqualified individuals, especially if demand greatly exceeds supply.

fied individuals, even as workers in that sector complain that there are not enough open positions. This can happen when employers seek talent with very particular skill requirements and balk at training or retraining potential hires. Rapid turnover, which is common in fast-moving high-tech fields, can also exacerbate perceived shortages, even when there are enough qualified workers in the labor pool. Another complication in measuring supply and demand is that the job categories used in the collection of statistics by the Department of Labor are not always well aligned with the occupation of interest. For example, as noted above, the "information security analysts" category does not necessarily include everyone who is a cybersecurity worker, and there may be cybersecurity workers who do not neatly fit into a single category.

The national origin of cybersecurity workers also affects supply. Firms without global reach must either rely on workers within the U.S. workforce or work within a complex system for hiring foreign workers. By contrast, firms with global operations are able to seek talent wherever it exists across the globe and move at least some cybersecurity work to where they find it. Firms of all sizes can outsource some or all of their cybersecurity work, and some of this may also be performed offshore. U.S. citizenship is generally required for federal government cybersecurity positions, and security clearance requirements for national security-related jobs further restrict the pool of candidates to U.S. citizens.

ROLES, RESPONSIBILITIES, AND CONTEXTS FOR CYBERSECURITY WORK

The cybersecurity workforce is quite diverse, encompassing a wide variety of roles and responsibilities, each involving an array of different skills and abilities. It includes workers in the private and nonprofit sector, military, and civilian government.

The diverse mix of skills in the cybersecurity workforce reflects the complex nature of cybersecurity. Some of the cybersecurity problem is technical (i.e., drawing on computer science techniques and skills), but given that cybersecurity is inherently concerned with human adversaries and the behaviors of those in the organizations that they target, behavioral and management aspects are also critical.

Effective response to an attack involves understanding and anticipating the actions of an attacker. As a result, in some jobs, an adversarial mindset and approach may be as important as the aggregation of particular technical skills in roles that involve detecting, tracking, or responding to an attack. Workshop participants noted that some of the most talented individuals in this context today are people who lack formal education, training, or certification—and that these individuals may be unwilling to pursue any of these to meet a hiring requirement. Indeed, it was clear from presentations and discussion at the workshops that such "self-taught" experts play key roles in some organizations.

Moreover, security capabilities are hard for end users, administrators, and developers to understand, making it all too easy to use, operate, or construct systems that are inadvertently insecure. Insights on how to address usability often come from the disciplines of human-computer interaction and psychology.[11] Behavioral expertise is relevant in efforts to detect and deter potential insider threats. Because failures to adopt, deploy, or use adequate cybersecurity measures often stem from insufficient incentives, the disciplines of economics, anthropology, and psychology are also relevant for cybersecurity.[12]

Given that many aspects of cybersecurity involve highly technical matters, it is often not appreciated that "soft skills" are also important, much as they are in other technical fields. These skills include the ability to work in teams and facility with oral and written communication. Response to an incident may require coordinating activities across multiple organizational elements or job functions and may involve interactions with vendors, security consultants, law enforcement, or other outside actors. Given the dynamic nature of the information technology substrate and threat environment, the ability to continue to learn is also important. All of these traits are at a particular premium in the often complex response to "advanced persistent threats," where adversaries possess sophisticated levels of expertise and significant resources that allow them to pursue their objectives through multiple attack vectors. Organizations confronting cybersecurity threats increasingly find themselves conducting what has been dubbed "cyber intelligence" in addition to more traditional cybersecurity activities.[13]

The organizational context in which the cybersecurity workforce is employed is also diverse. For example, the cybersecurity capabilities of employers vary considerably and include the following:

- *Employers with large, specialized cybersecurity operations* that have built up a cadre of highly skilled, extensively trained specialists who work together on the most complex cybersecurity problems. Such organizations

---

[11] National Research Council, *Toward Better Usability, Security, and Privacy of Information Technology: Report of a Workshop,* The National Academies Press, Washington, D.C., 2010.

[12] Ross Anderson and Tyler Moore, Information security: Where computer science, economics and psychology meet, *Philosophical Transactions of the Royal Society A: Mathematical, Physical and Engineering Sciences* 367(1898):2717-2727, 2009; ibid.

[13] Troy Townsend et al. *Emerging Technology Center Report: Cyber Intelligence Tradecraft Project Summary of Key Findings,* Software Engineering Institute, Carnegie Mellon University, Pittsburgh, Pa., 2013.

are characterized by willingness and ability to make the necessary investments and by having management with sufficient savvy to identify and recruit high-caliber talent.
- *Employers with mixed cybersecurity groups* that employ more than one security specialist, typically led by a manager who is knowledgeable but not necessarily expert in the field.
- *Employers with distributed cybersecurity functions*, in which cybersecurity is the responsibility of a general information technology (IT) worker or manager as part of a broader IT job, typically performed in contexts where managers have little specialized knowledge or understanding of cybersecurity.

In the first case, organizations with global reach may send work offshore to wherever expertise can be found within the enterprise. In the second two cases, organizations will rely, at least in part, on outsourced work to obtain the necessary expertise, and some of this work may be offshored by the firm providing the security services.

As is true in many fields, there are varying approaches to how work is divided between the cybersecurity workforce and the broader workforce, because the lines between cybersecurity and other roles are blurry, reflecting overlaps in both expertise and responsibility. For example, when a change is made to address a cybersecurity problem, someone designated as having cybersecurity responsibilities may recommend a configuration change that is, in turn, implemented by a network engineer who is not designated as a cybersecurity employee. Also, high-level decisions about investment in cybersecurity may be made by individuals who have risk management responsibilities that extend well beyond cybersecurity. Another example is privacy, where issues, technical approaches, and job responsibilities often overlap with cybersecurity.

Because attacks can cross international borders, cybersecurity work sometimes has an international dimension. Cybersecurity work may involve coordinating activities in multiple countries and thus require the ability to work with international counterparts from both the private sector and other governments and the knowledge and skills to properly comply with rules and policies that can differ by jurisdiction. For example, cybersecurity work sometimes involves use of sensitive information about vulnerabilities and responses.

In short, cybersecurity work encompasses a wide range of roles and contexts, and there are many different ways to classify cybersecurity work. Some workshop participants commented that agreement on a common framework would be helpful in understanding and developing the cybersecurity workforce, and this view prompted the commissioning of such a framework under the National Initiative for Cybersecurity Education (NICE). Issued by the National Institute for Standards and Technology, the recently released NICE framework divides cybersecurity roles into high-level areas of specialization, each of which contains multiple subspecialties.[14] Today, this framework is being referenced as part of workforce development efforts in parts of the federal government and, to a lesser extent, in the private sector. Some workshop participants cited the framework as a helpful or much needed development; others observed that it did not seem relevant, given how they currently thought about the structure of their organization's workforce.

FACTORS AFFECTING FUTURE CYBERSECURITY WORKFORCE NEEDS

It is even more difficult to assess future need, demand, and supply for cybersecurity (or information technology more broadly). There are many indications today that demand will continue to be high. For example, the Bureau of Labor Statistics estimates a faster-than-average growth rate in employment for the decade 2010 to 2020 of "information security analysts," a labor category that represents a significant subset of the cybersecurity workforce.[15] In a 2012 survey of information security professionals, more than half reported that their organizations had too few information security workers.[16]

There are a number of factors that could increase or decrease the needed capacity in particular areas or affect the needed workforce capabilities, including the following:

- *How the cybersecurity challenge will evolve as new technologies and threats emerge and old threats evolve, and what the resulting workforce requirements will be.* At least historically, new technologies have been deployed without sufficient attention to the security implications, and bad actors have found ways to exploit the resulting vulnerabilities. Familiar examples include the introduction of networked personal computers into the workplace and widespread adoption of the Internet for mission-critical activities.
- *What the key skills and best practices will be in cybersecurity, and what the content of curricula should be,* because the ability to build more secure

---

[14] National Institute for Standards and Technology, U.S. Department of Commerce, *National Cybersecurity Workforce Framework*, Washington, D.C., 2013.

[15] National Center for O*NET Development, Bureau of Labor Statistics, O*Net Online Summary Report for 15-1122.00—Information Security Analysts, 2013, available at http://www.onetonline.org/link/summary/15-1122.00.

[16] Michael Suby, *The 2013 (ISC)² Global Information Security Workforce Study*, Frost and Sullivan, Mountain View, Calif., 2013.

systems lags what is needed, and knowledge about how to protect, defend, and repair computer systems continues to grow.

- *How advances on various fronts might affect the mix of needed capacity and capability.* For example, better software design and development from a security perspective would result in fewer vulnerabilities to be exploited (and thus potentially require fewer people to detect, patch, and respond), better tools and techniques for cybersecurity might reduce the number of workers needed in certain roles and change the skills needed for others, more robust law enforcement action might reduce the incidence of certain forms of cybercrime, better training and understanding of security among system administrators would enable them to better "harden" systems, and better training of the workers that operate systems would help them avoid actions that undermine security. In the case of better tools and techniques that enhance productivity, it is possible that demand for workers might shift to higher-end positions, because fewer workers would be needed to carry out functions that are partly or fully automated. Emerging technologies like cloud services could enhance security by reducing the burden on individual organizations, but it could also introduce new risks by changing the boundary of an organization's information systems.

- *How the policy environment for cybersecurity will change.* For example, if new cybersecurity or privacy regulations were introduced, organizations would need to increase their workforce to comply with the new requirements and document and report on compliance.

- *How cybersecurity will be provided in the future, especially in smaller organizations.* Already, many organizations turn to vendors to supply various cybersecurity tools and services, and there are models in which cybersecurity work can be outsourced to service providers. For example, Internet service providers increasingly offer a range of security services for their customers. In the increasingly popular software-as-a-service model, vendors generally take responsibility for configuration, monitoring, and response. Such shifts of duties may reduce the number or change the mix of cybersecurity workers needed by organizations. On the other hand, every organization that uses IT will need people who can take responsibility for the organization's cybersecurity, at a minimum being able to select vendors that can provide the required levels of assurance. Future trends in offshoring security work will also affect the demand for U.S. cybersecurity workers.

2

Approaches to Professionalization

PROFESSION

Profession has multiple interpretations, ranging from the common use of the word to more formal definitions that spell out the various elements generally associated with the establishment of a profession. The common meaning of profession is "a paid occupation, especially one that involves prolonged training and a formal qualification."[1]

A useful, more comprehensive definition can be derived from suggestions by several speakers at the workshops convened by this committee. That definition identifies the following characteristics of a professional: (1) passing a knowledge and/or performance test, (2) superior completion of study of intellectual basis of the profession, (3) a sustained period of mentored experience/apprenticeship, (4) continuing education, (5) licensing by a formal authority, and (6) ethical standards of behavior with enforcement, including removal from profession.[2] A field that possesses

---

[1] *New Oxford American Dictionary*, third edition, Oxford University Press, 2010.

[2] Many similar definitions or subsets of this definition appear in the literature. For example, white papers prepared for the National Initiative on Cybersecurity Education use a definition with three elements (a body of knowledge, ethical guidelines, and professional organization that publishes papers and establishes best practices) (Department of Homeland Security, National Initiative for Cybersecurity Education, "The Path toward Cybersecurity Professionalization: Insights from Other Occupations: White Paper," 2012, available at http://niccs.us-cert.gov/careers/professionalization). The definition used in this report was presented by Franklin Reeder in his remarks at the committee's December 13, 2012, workshop.

all of these characteristics will almost certainly be recognized as a profession, but not all are required for a field to be recognized as a profession. This broader definition illustrates the different mechanisms for professionalization that might be applied to cybersecurity work.

PROFESSIONALIZATION

Professionalization describes (1) education, training, and other activities that transform a worker into a professional and (2) social processes by which an occupation becomes a profession. Although cybersecurity concerns have existed from the earliest days of shared and networked computers, and there have long been workers responsible for various aspects of computer and network security, it has taken some time for the view of cybersecurity as a distinct occupational field, replete with many subspecialties, to emerge.

Today, a growing number of workers think of themselves as cybersecurity professionals based on their job roles, experience, and expertise, and an array of government and private sector entities are pursuing activities related to professionalization. Professional societies in computer science, computer engineering, and cybersecurity have worked to develop bodies of knowledge and instituted codes of ethics.[3] Multiple federal agencies, notably the Department of Defense and the Department of Homeland Security (DHS), the National Security Agency (NSA), and the Office of Personnel Management, have workforce development activities under way. A growing number of educational institutions offer degrees or specializations in cybersecurity, and a National Centers of Academic Excellence program, sponsored by NSA and DHS, certifies education, training, and research programs of 2- and 4-year academic institutions against standards established jointly by those two federal agencies.

A sufficiently large number of certificates and certifications in various cybersecurity skills and specializations have emerged that DHS has developed a searchable online catalog to guide workers and employers.[4] These include general certifications like the Certified Information Systems Security Professional (CISSP) as well as many specialized certifications. A variety of organizations within and outside the government either require or encourage certification for certain job roles. For example, Department

---

[3] These include the Association for Computing Machinery's "Code of Ethics and Professional Conduct," the IEEE Computer Society's "Software Engineering Code of Ethics and Professional Practice," and the International Information Systems Security Certification Consortium's "Code of Ethics."

[4] U.S. Department of Homeland Security, Professional Certifications, available at http://niccs.us-cert.gov/training/professional-certifications.

of Defense Directive 8570[5] requires CISSP certification of department personnel who perform information assurance functions.[6]

Professionalization can be a bottom-up process driven by those in the occupation, a top-down process driven by employers or the government (as an employer or as a policy maker), or some combination of the two. For an employer, professionalization might mean encouraging or requiring a particular course of academic study, degree, certificate, certification, or professional society membership as a condition of initial and/or continuing employment. For a professional association, professionalization might mean establishing a code of conduct or creating (or recognizing) certifications, training programs, or educational standards. For the government, professionalization might mean encouraging or requiring a particular educational achievement or certifications for its own workforce, supporting the development of curricula, establishing standards for education programs, encouraging the use of certification as a means of regulating the workers whose jobs affect the health and safety or property of others, or requiring (at either the federal or state level) licensure for particular occupations.

GOALS FOR PROFESSIONALIZATION

Historically, professionalization has had one or more of the following goals: (1) to establish standards that enhance the quality of the workforce; (2) to regulate workers whose jobs can affect the health, safety, or property of others; (3) to enhance public trust and confidence; (4) to enable compliance with regulatory or legal requirements; (5) to enhance the status of an occupation; (6) to establish a monopoly or otherwise regulate the supply of labor to advance the interests of its members; (7) to guide the behavior of practitioners in the field, especially when it comes to morally or ethically ambiguous activities; or (8) to establish and standardize roles (and the associated knowledge, skills, and abilities) and pathways so as to better align supply and demand, increase awareness of career paths, and facilitate recruitment and retention by employers.[7]

An additional, often unstated but important, goal is to establish a shared set of values, culture, ethos, and mindset for a profession. These

---

[5] Department of Defense, *DOD 8570.01-M: Information Assurance Workforce Improvement*, Washington, D.C., 2012.

[6] As of this writing, the Department of Defense is reevaluating certification requirements. Zachary Fryer-Biggs, Experts say DoD workers undertrained, *Federal Times*, February 16, 2013.

[7] This set of goals draws on observations offered by workshop participants and includes elements commonly found in the literature on professionalization. See, for example, W.J. Orlikowski, and J.J. Baroudi, The information systems profession: Myth or reality?, *Information Technology and People* 4(1):13-30, 1988.

commonalities can contribute to people's ability to work together effectively, particularly across roles within an organization and across organizations.

SPECIFIC MECHANISMS FOR PROFESSIONALIZATION AND HOW THEY AFFECT WORKFORCE CAPACITY AND CAPABILITY

Codes of Conduct or Ethics

Codes of conduct or ethics fall into two types: (1) enforceable codes whose breach can lead to revocation of a certification, or even removal from the profession, and (2) nonenforceable codes that are generally associated with membership in a professional society. Although workshop participants did not cite examples of where ethical violations had been an issue, more than one participant observed that some cybersecurity workers are placed in positions that involve significant responsibility and trust. A possible concern with such codes is how they affect the recruitment of "black hats" (i.e., those who have violated computer security laws or rules in the past) into "white hat" jobs. This issue is likely to recede over time as the supply of qualified workers grows, reducing the need to hire those with criminal or otherwise less trustworthy backgrounds. Another issue is that some specialized cybersecurity jobs that involve offensive operations or active defense might run afoul of codes that do not take such work into account, a tension that other fields have had to consider in developing their ethical standards.

Education

Education for cybersecurity is provided at the undergraduate level by both 2- and 4-year institutions, which offer a wide range of courses, programs, and degrees focused on cybersecurity and as a component of computer science and engineering, management information system, and other information technology (IT)-related courses, programs, and degrees. Cybersecurity education can also be provided in non-IT contexts, such as in business or public policy programs.

Certificates and Certifications

Certificates are generally associated with training or education courses and verify through examination that particular content was learned in courses or curricula. They are generally "good for life" and cannot be revoked, although a certificate's relevance to an employer will diminish over time, especially in a fast-moving field like cybersecurity. They serve as an indication of knowledge at a particular point in time.

Certification is a formal procedure by an authorized or accredited body.[8] It is based on a study of the factors that predict success in a job and relies on examinations that meet testing standards. Certifications are time limited and require periodic recertification, and there are procedures in place to remove certification for ethical breaches or knowledge deficiencies. Certification can also be applied to the content of education and training programs as well as individuals. The Centers for Academic Excellence programs described above certifies that the education, training, and research programs meet an external standard.

A challenge associated with developing or updating a certification is that it takes time to reach consensus on the knowledge and skills to be assessed. This creates challenges in an area like cybersecurity where the underlying technologies, threats, and context are fast moving. One risk is obsolescence—the knowledge or skills tested for are out-of-date by the time the certification is issued. Another risk is ossification—when the establishment of a standard inhibits evolution of skills and knowledge because those certified may not be incentivized to learn beyond what was included in the last certification test. Organizations that offer certifications can address these challenges by focusing assessments as much as possible on fundamental concepts, by adopting nimble processes for updating content, and by requiring periodic recertification. Continuing education is especially important, both in the context of certifications and more broadly for the workforce, given the rapid rate of change in cybersecurity knowledge.

Certificates and certifications are especially helpful to employers who may find it otherwise difficult to evaluate the skills and knowledge of job applicants, especially small organizations that do not have a hiring manager with deep cybersecurity expertise.[9] Even in these cases, certificates and certifications may not be dispositive but may be given greater weight. In addition to providing evidence of competence, certificates and certifications may be useful indicators of interest and commitment to work in a field and provide a useful complement or supplement to academic degrees in establishing knowledge and commitment.

A number of workshop participants observed that some certifications play a useful role in helping employers determine that an applicant has been exposed to a minimum level of knowledge. CISSP certification is

---

[8] The distinction between certificates and certifications is reflected in American National Standards Institute, "Assessment Based Certificate Programs," ANSI/NOCA Standard 1100, 2009. The definitions used here are drawn from a presentation at the March 28, 2013, workshop, by Roy Swift, American National Standards Institute.

[9] As observed above, another possibility for such organizations is to outsource cybersecurity work (e.g., consultants) or outsource some of the responsibility (e.g., via software as a service).

a canonical example. Others observed that many qualified and, indeed, very highly qualified applicants can be found who do not have a CISSP or other certification, and so requiring such certification would undesirably restrict the candidate pool.

Views expressed by workshop participants with respect to the value of certificates and certifications in the context of their own careers or workplaces varied. Some indicated that certificates and certifications had helped advance their careers and/or were perceived as valuable credentials within their organizations. Other participants observed that certificates and certifications were not viewed so positively in some contexts—that other factors, such as experience, demonstrated ability, or educational achievement, were seen as better measures. A few said that they sometimes omitted listing them on their resumes for this reason.

Certificates and certifications also play a role in establishing the qualifications and credibility of those who testify in court, and thus it is no surprise that several certifications in digital forensics are now offered. Interestingly, at the committee's December 2012 workshop, participants from two federal government organizations described entirely different approaches to certification of forensic experts. One sought to have all of the organization's experts certified to enhance the experts' credibility in court, while the other discouraged certification out of concern that a capable expert might for some reason not pass a particular certification exam and that this fact could be used to question the expert's court testimony irrespective of the expert's actual knowledge and skills.

Licensure

Licensure involves a government restriction on practice without a license, generally involving public safety or trust. It may establish standards for legal liability in the case of negligent practice. In engineering fields, a small fraction of workers with degrees in engineering fields are licensed as professional engineers. For example, a licensed civil engineer responsible for approving a bridge design is assumed to be able to state with some certainty that the bridge will stand under stated conditions. By contrast, for software and security no equivalent knowledge exists, which is one reason that licensure has not taken hold in the related area of software engineering. Also, cybersecurity is carried out in an adversarial environment where human behavior plays a central role. As a result, it likely is too early for licensure in cybersecurity, at least broadly, but the approach may have some utility in the future as the underlying science and engineering practice improves.

TIMESCALES FOR PROFESSIONALIZATION

The path toward professionalization of an occupation is generally a long one, and debates about the best approach can continue for decades. There has, for example, been a multi-decade discussion about professionalization of software engineering, with no consensus as yet reached among workers, professional organizations, and employers. In that regard, for example, the Association for Computing Machinery has taken a public position that is unfavorable to licensing of software engineers, while the Institute of Electrical and Electronics Engineers has been more receptive. Today, only one state, Texas, recognizes professional software engineers, and the software industry remains largely "policed" by the marketplace.

Even in a field as old as medicine, professionalization has continued to evolve. More than 100 years ago, the Flexner report[10] spurred education reforms and greater professionalization of medical practice. Professionalization mechanisms in medicine have also seen significant evolution during this time. For example, medicine has increasingly been subdivided into distinct specialty roles (e.g., the emergence of board-certified specialties and subspecialties) that have made it easier to identify specific certification criteria in the face of expanding and evolving knowledge and skill requirements. Even today, debate about how the necessary skills and knowledge for medical students are best acquired through classroom education and hands-on practice continues, reflecting the growing body of scientific knowledge, the increasing complexity of clinical care, and the evolving socioeconomic context in which medicine is practiced.[11] An important and open question is whether cybersecurity will endure in anything like its present form over the timescales in which professionalization emerged and matured in professions like medicine, law, and aviation.

TRADE-OFFS ASSOCIATED WITH PROFESSIONALIZATION

Chapter 1 described some of the uncertainties associated with the current and future supply and demand for cybersecurity workers and the diversity of contexts in which cybersecurity work is done. This chapter has outlined the range of potential professionalization measures and some of the associated advantages and disadvantages. Taking these together,

---

[10] A. Flexner, *Medical Education in the United States and Canada: A Report to the Carnegie Foundation for the Advancement of Teaching*, Merrymount Press, Boston, Mass., 1910.

[11] There is a rich literature on the future of medical education and the recommendations of the Flexner report. See, for example, M. Cooke, D.M. Irby, W. Sullivan, and K.M. Ludmerer, "American medical education 100 years after the Flexner Report," *New England Journal of Medicine* 355(13):1339-1344, 2006.

the committee identified a set of trade-offs associated with actions to professionalize the cybersecurity workforce. These include the following:

- *Quality versus quantity.* Improvements in quality that can be shown to result from professionalization mechanisms should be weighed against supply restrictions that the resulting additional barriers to entry would create. Professionalization can be both a funnel (restricting people from entering the field) and a magnet (attracting people to the field). It can also act as a sieve if people who moved from general IT or other positions into cybersecurity roles find themselves subject to new professionalization requirements and then move out of cybersecurity. This tension comes into play when employers expect job candidates to already have experience and credentials, rather than investing in on-the-job training. The time and cost associated with obtaining the required education, training, experience, and credentials will discourage some from entering the field.
- *Standardization versus dynamism.* The value of standardization associated with development of common curricula or certifications should be weighed against the time it takes to reach consensus on standards, given the rate of change in underlying technologies, the introduction of new technologies, and the rapid pace at which the context and threat evolve. In other words, the benefits of standardization should be weighed against the risks of obsolescence (the knowledge or skills associated with the standard are out-of-date) and ossification (the establishment of a standard inhibits evolution of skills and knowledge).
- *Broad versus niche needs.* Given the great diversity of roles, responsibilities, and contexts, the fact that professionalization measures (e.g., certification) may be warranted in a particular subfield and context (e.g., digital forensics) should not be confused with a broad need for professionalization.
- *Better information for employers versus false certainty.* Certificates and certifications provide some ability to vet job candidates, but overreliance on them may screen out some of the most talented and suitable individuals. This is particularly true in cybersecurity, in which some of the most proficient cyber experts have developed their skill sets through informal methods (e.g., self-taught hackers). Organizations that do not already have a sophisticated cybersecurity workforce may place a greater value on professionalization measures, which make it easier for them to identify qualified workers. However, at a time when few think the cybersecurity situation is improving, out-of-the-box thinking may be at a premium but may be lost with overly rigid screening.
- *Certainty about worker capabilities versus uncertainty about actual job requirements.* Increased certainty about the capabilities of a professional that may result from professionalization should be weighed against the

uncertainty about what skills, knowledge, or abilities are actually needed in a particular role and uncertainty about how roles may change as the technological, organizational, and threat context evolves.

- *Specificity versus flexibility.* Employers and their hiring managers and human resource staff will seek sufficient specificity to assure that a candidate has the right set of skills and abilities for a position. They may also seek specificity simply to make it easier to identify candidates (although at the risk of overlooking candidates who may be suitable but lack the specified qualifications). At the same time, job boundaries are never firm, and in the evolving world of cybersecurity, roles and needs can be especially fluid, which means that enough flexibility to select candidates who are more broadly suited for that range of possible roles is also important.
- *Stimulation of supply and better matching of supply to demand versus restriction of supply.* Professionalization may increase supply over time as it helps increase awareness and desirability of a profession and thus increases the number of individuals who consider cybersecurity as a career. By helping define roles and career paths, professionalization can help workers identify suitable jobs and employers identify suitable workers. On the other hand, defining the field in terms of a specific set of exams, certificates, degrees, or the like will narrow the pipeline of future candidates for the field and thus may constrain supply.

The committee believes that careful consideration of these trade-offs will help inform decision-making by employers, professional organizations, and governments about whether and how to undertake activities to professionalize the cybersecurity workforce. They do not represent "either/or" choices, but trade-offs to be weighed. Conclusion 7 of this report presents these trade-offs as questions to pose about any given professionalization effort.

3

Conclusions, Recommendation, and Criteria for Professionalization of Cybersecurity

This report considers the role that professionalization might play in ensuring that the United States has enough cybersecurity workers (capacity) and that it has a workforce with the right knowledge, skills, and abilities (capability). These issues arise at a critical juncture, when there is growing recognition that the cybersecurity threat is serious and pervasive. Where and how professionalization would contribute to, or possibly diminish, the capacity and capability of the national workforce to provide cybersecurity are questions that do not have a simple or single answer.

CAPACITY AND CAPABILITY OF THE CYBERSECURITY WORKFORCE

Conclusion 1. More attention to both the capacity and capability of the U.S. cybersecurity workforce is needed.

Even large organizations with top talent and significant resources devoted to cybersecurity have suffered major cybersecurity compromises, and organizations that do not have such levels of talent or resources face even greater challenges. More highly skilled workers in cybersecurity roles would help the nation respond more robustly to the cybersecurity problems it faces. All organizations need to understand their threat environment and the risks they face, address their cybersecurity problems, and hire the most appropriate people to do that work.

Conclusion 2. Although the need for cybersecurity workers is likely to continue to be high, it is difficult to forecast with certainty the number of workers required or the needed mix of cybersecurity knowledge and skills.

There are many indications today that demand for cybersecurity workers will continue to be high, but it is notoriously difficult to measure or forecast labor supply and demand for any field, especially one that is as dynamic and fast moving as cybersecurity. Moreover, there are several factors that may affect future need. These include the following:

- How the cybersecurity challenge will evolve as technologies and threats evolve, and how this may alter workforce capability and capacity requirements.
- How advances—such as better-quality, more-secure software; more productive cybersecurity tools; better training of the workers that operate and manage IT systems; or more robust law enforcement—might change the number of workers needed in certain roles and change the skills needed for others.
- How much responsibility for cybersecurity might shift from organizations at large to more specialist information technology (IT) or cybersecurity firms, which may reduce the number or change the mix of cybersecurity workers needed by organizations.

CYBERSECURITY WORK AND THE CYBERSECURITY WORKFORCE

Conclusion 3. The cybersecurity workforce encompasses a variety of contexts, roles, and occupations and is too broad and diverse to be treated as a single occupation or profession. Whether and how to professionalize will vary according to role and context.

Cybersecurity is a field that encompasses more than one kind of work and more than one occupation or profession. Some kinds of workers may come to be considered as professionals, but the committee believes that the field may also include a range of personnel and functions that are best not considered as professionals, much as many other fields contain both professionals and other workers who are not formally professionalized, including some who are designated as paraprofessionals. For example, there are today large numbers of people within organizations who have responsibility for cybersecurity functions, such as frontline IT support staff, for whom there may not be any formal education or accreditation requirements. The organizational context for cybersecurity work is diverse, ranging from firms that have highly proficient cybersecurity groups to ones where cybersecurity is one of the responsibilities of general IT groups. There are also varying approaches to how work is divided between the cybersecurity workforce and the broader IT workforce—some cybersecurity positions are clearly hybrid in nature, blending cybersecurity roles with other roles in IT, management, or law enforcement.

The committee heard a wide range of opinions regarding the contexts in which professionalization would or would not be appropriate. The committee noted only one case where there is a compelling and widely agreed-on case for professionalization today. In digital forensics, where the results are to be used in a legal proceeding, the work is comparatively narrowly defined by procedures and law, the relevant domain of expertise appears to be sufficiently narrow, and the appropriate professionalization mechanism is clear (certification with periodic recertification reflecting advances in acceptable forensic techniques and practices). Even in this case, however, the committee learned that not all agencies that employ digital forensics examiners currently favor external certification.

Given the great diversity of roles, responsibilities, and contexts, the fact that professionalization measures may be warranted in a particular subfield and context should not be confused with a broad need for professionalization. Those organizations that find professionalization helpful can certainly insist on some form of certification or other professionalization measure for the workers they hire, and a number of organizations inside and outside government do so today. Other organizations, having given this serious thought, may find other ways to optimize and customize their hiring and cybersecurity workforce composition to best meet their specific needs.

Professionalizing by roles, which are the building blocks of professional categories, would be at too low a level. At the same time, it would be a mistake to attempt to professionalize at too high a level—for example, by identifying a single set of professional requirements for multiple, distinct occupations (with different knowledge requirements) within a broad field.

Conclusion 4. Because cybersecurity is not solely a technical endeavor, a wide range of backgrounds and skills will be needed in an effective national cybersecurity workforce.

For example:

• Attackers target organizations and individuals as well as machines and networks, so cybersecurity is inherently concerned with human adversaries and behaviors of those in the organizations they target. Protecting cyberspace thus involves human, behavioral, psychological, and economic factors and management expertise as well as technical skills and knowledge.

- Cybersecurity is a function of organizational policies and process as well as technologies. As a result, people are needed who understand the organizational context—mission requirements, business processes, and organizational culture.
- Cybersecurity work often involves teamwork and collaboration across organizational boundaries. Soft skills, which include the ability to work in teams and facility with oral and written communication, are essential in many roles.

As a result, education, training, and workforce development activities that focus too much on narrow technical knowledge and skills may discourage participation by people with much-needed nontechnical knowledge and skills, may overly concentrate attention and resources on building technical capability and capacity, and may discourage technically proficient people from developing nontechnical skills. The result would fall short of delivering the workforce the nation requires.

PROFESSIONALIZATION

Conclusion 5. Professionalization has multiple goals and can occur through multiple mechanisms.

"Professionalization" describes the social process by which an occupation becomes a profession. Its goals include establishing quality standards, enhancing public trust and confidence, and establishing and standardizing job roles and pathways. The movement toward the professionalization of an occupation has multiple goals and can occur through multiple mechanisms. Members of a nascent profession may seek to establish a monopoly or otherwise regulate the supply of labor to advance their interests. An additional and often unstated but important goal is to establish a shared set of values, ethos, standards of conduct, culture, and mindset for a profession. Another frequently unstated goal is to facilitate compliance with contractual or other requirements.

Professional status for an individual is generally associated with the following mechanisms: (1) passing a knowledge and/or performance test, (2) completion of a course of study on the intellectual basis of the profession, (3) a sustained period of mentored experience/apprenticeship, (4) continuing education, (5) licensing by a formal authority, and (6) ethical standards of behavior with enforcement. A field in which all of these mechanisms are used will almost certainly be recognized as a profession, but not all are required for a field to be recognized as a profession.

The committee made several observations regarding the role and application of several of these mechanisms:

- *Codes of conduct or ethics* define the norms of behavior for a profession. Although the adoption of such codes is generally a positive step with few drawbacks, it does raise two possible concerns in the context of cybersecurity. One issue is how the codes relate to actions taken in roles that involve offensive operations or active defensive measures (where legitimate activities might run afoul of overly narrowly drawn standards). The other is how the codes might (in the short run) affect the hiring of "black hats" (those who have violated computer security laws or rules in the past but may be a valuable source of talent in protecting computer security) for "white hat" jobs.[1]
- *Certificates* and *certification* are ways to demonstrate not only an individual's competence in a well-defined area of cybersecurity, but also an individual's interest and commitment. They may provide a useful complement or supplement to academic degrees in establishing knowledge and commitment. Views of certificates and certifications vary with respect to individual careers or workplaces: some see them as valuable, while others omit them from resumes because they believe they may diminish, not enhance, some employers' perception of their technical credentials. The content of education and training programs can also be certified to have met an external standard.
- *Licensure* involves a government restriction on practice without a license, generally for reasons involving public safety or trust. The sense of the committee is that it is too early for licensure in cybersecurity, at least broadly, because today's engineering practices for cybersecurity fall short of highly reliable methodologies found in some other areas of engineering where licensing has been applied. Licensure may have some utility in the future as the underlying science and engineering practice improves.

Conclusion 6. The path toward professionalization of a field can be slow and difficult, and not all portions of a field can or should be professionalized at the same time.

There has, for example, been a multi-decade discussion about the professionalization of software developers, with no consensus as yet reached

---

[1] There are other contexts, such as law enforcement and the military, where a careful distinction must be made between actions that may be duty in one context but prohibited, or even criminal, in another.

among workers, professional organizations, and employers about whether or how to professionalize. Even 100 years after the Flexner report,[2] which spurred education reforms and greater professionalization of medical practice, the medical profession continues to debate how best to instill new doctors with the requisite knowledge and skills. The professionalization of other fields, such as law and aviation, has also evolved over the course of many decades. Where professionalization does occur, it will take time, as consensus is developed, professional associations emerge or evolve, and professionalization mechanisms achieve recognition by employers and government.

CRITERIA

Conclusion 7. Professionalization has associated costs and benefits that should be weighed when making decisions to undertake professionalization activities.

Professionalization is not a proxy for "better," but it may be a useful tool in certain circumstances. The following criteria are suggested to help identify cybersecurity specialties and circumstances where professionalization may be appropriate and to assess the potential effects of different professionalization mechanisms:

• *Do the benefits of a given professionalization measure outweigh the potential supply restrictions resulting from the additional barriers to entry?* Professionalization can be both a magnet (attracting people to the field) and a funnel (restricting people from entering the field). It can also act as a sieve if people who have moved from general IT occupations or other positions into cybersecurity roles are subjected to new professionalization requirements and then move out of cybersecurity. The cost and time required for certification or a degree may also narrow the pipeline of people entering the field. A corollary is that overly narrow professionalization measures may filter out workers whose skills are needed (e.g., certifications focused on technical skills that filter out needed nontechnical skills). On the other hand, professionalization may increase supply over time, as it helps increase awareness and desirability of that profession and thus increases the number of individuals who consider cybersecurity as a career. By helping define roles and career paths, it can also help workers identify suitable jobs and help employers identify suitable workers. Specialization and stratification may also help address supply issues, much as the

---

[2] A. Flexner, *Medical Education in the United States and Canada: A Report to the Carnegie Foundation for the Advancement of Teaching*, Merrymount Press, Boston, Mass., 1910.

introduction of nurse practitioners and physician assistants expanded the workforce providing primary medical care.

- *Does the potential to provide additional information about a candidate outweigh the risks of false certainty about who is actually best suited for a job?* Certificates and certifications may provide useful tools for vetting job candidates, but overreliance on them may screen out some of the most talented and suitable individuals. This is particularly true in cybersecurity today, where some of the most effective workers develop their skillsets through informal methods (e.g., self-taught hackers). Organizations that do not already have a sophisticated cybersecurity workforce may place a greater value on professionalization measures because they make it easier for them to identify qualified workers. However, at a time when few think the cybersecurity situation is improving, and where "sideways" thinking may be at a premium, creativity and innovation may be lost with overly rigid screening. Moreover, given the fluid and changing nature of cybersecurity work, the knowledge, skills, and abilities actually needed in a particular job can change, and workers' roles and responsibilities can also shift rapidly.

- *Do the benefits of establishing the standards needed for professionalization outweigh the risks of obsolescence (when the knowledge or skills associated with the standard are out-of-date by the time a standard is agreed on) and ossification (when the establishment of a standard inhibits further development by workers of their skills and knowledge)?* It takes time to reach consensus on the standards needed to establish a curriculum or certification, and it can be difficult to reach convergence, given the rate of change in underlying technologies and the rapid pace at which the context and threat evolve. Following receipt of a degree or certification, workers may stop developing their skills and knowledge. Strategies for addressing these challenges include focusing assessments as much as possible on fundamental concepts, segmenting a field (where possible) into sufficiently narrow specialty roles, adopting more nimble processes for updating content, and requiring continuing education and periodic recertification to refresh requirements.

> **Recommendation. Activities by the federal government and other entities to professionalize a cybersecurity occupation should be undertaken only when that occupation has well-defined and stable characteristics, when there are observed deficiencies in the occupational workforce that professionalization could help remedy, and when the benefits outweigh the costs.**

Cybersecurity is a broad field, and professionalization is something that can be undertaken for specific occupations within the field and not the field as a whole. Before professionalization activities are undertaken for an occupation, two high-level criteria should be met:

1. *The occupation has well-defined characteristics.* These include the following:

- Stable knowledge and skill requirements. The occupation should have a stable (but not necessarily static) common body of knowledge on which members of the profession can be judged to a generally agreed-upon standard. This does not imply, however, that the occupation is static; even within a rapidly evolving profession, core knowledge elements that remain stable can be identified.
- Stable roles and responsibilities and occupational boundaries that distinguish the profession from others.
- Well-defined career ladders that provide links to professionalization mechanisms.
- Agreed-upon ethical standards to which members of the profession will be held.

Not all of these characteristics or standards must be met, but the level of readiness for professionalization is higher when more of them are met.

2. *There is credible evidence of deficiencies in the occupational workforce.* These might include skill deficiencies, questions of legitimacy among the current set of practitioners, or concerns about accountability. Each deficiency should be separately identified. There should be a compelling argument that professionalization (and the specific proposed mechanisms) will remedy each observed deficiency. Finally, the benefits of professionalization to remedy the targeted deficiencies should outweigh the potential costs.

Appendixes

Appendix A

Biographies of Committee Members

Diana L. Burley, *Co-Chair*, is associate professor in the Graduate School of Education and Human Development at George Washington University (GW). Dr. Burley joined GW in 2007 and has served as the inaugural chair of the Human and Organizational Learning Department and as director of the Executive Leadership Doctoral Program. Prior to joining the GW faculty, she served as a program officer in the Directorate for Education and Human Resources at the National Science Foundation (NSF), where she managed multimillion-dollar grant programs designed to increase the capacity of the U.S. higher education enterprise to produce scientists. At NSF she served as the lead program officer of the Federal Cyber Service Scholarship (Cyber Corps) program, and based on her work, Dr. Burley was honored by the Federal Chief Information Officers Council and the Colloquium on Information Systems Security Education for outstanding efforts toward the development of the federal cybersecurity workforce. She is a frequent contributor to the national cybersecurity forums, such as the National Initiative on Cyber Security Education (NICE) Workshop, the Federal Information Systems Security Educators' Association Conference, and the Department of Homeland Security's (DHS's) Software Assurance Forum. Most recently, Dr. Burley was appointed to the 2012 Commonwealth of Virginia Joint Commission on Technology and Science Cyber Security Committee. In addition, she serves as the co-principal investigator (co-PI) for Curriculum and Research of National CyberWatch, an NSF-funded cybersecurity research and education center. She is one of two GW representatives to the Institute for Information Infrastructure Protection

(I3P)—a consortium of leading institutions dedicated to strengthening the cyber infrastructure of the United States; a research scholar in the GW Institute for Public Policy; and a senior research scientist in the GW Cyber Security Research and Policy Institute. She holds an M.S. in public management and policy, an M.S. in organization science, and a Ph.D. in organization science and information technology from Carnegie Mellon University, where she studied as a Woodrow Wilson Foundation fellow in public policy.

Seymour (Sy) E. Goodman, *Co-Chair*, is professor of international affairs and computing, jointly at the Sam Nunn School of International Affairs and the College of Computing at the Georgia Institute of Technology (Georgia Tech). He serves as co-director of both the Georgia Tech Information Security Center and the Center for International Strategy, Technology and Policy. Dr. Goodman's research interests include international developments in the information technologies (IT), technology diffusion, IT and national security, and related public policy issues. Areas of geographic interest include the former Soviet Union and Eastern Europe, Latin America, the Middle East, South and Southeast Asia, and parts of Africa. Earlier research had been in areas of statistical and continuum physics, combinatorial algorithms, and software engineering. Current work includes research on the global diffusion of the Internet and the protection of large IT-based infrastructures. Immediately before coming to Georgia Tech, he was director of the Consortium for Research on Information Security and Policy at the Center for International Security and Cooperation, with an appointment in the Department of Engineering Economic Systems and Operations Research, both at Stanford University; and professor of management information systems and a member of the Center for Middle Eastern Studies at the University of Arizona. Earlier tenured and visiting appointments have been at the University of Virginia (applied mathematics, computer science, and Soviet and East European studies), Princeton University (mathematics and the Woodrow Wilson School of Public and International Affairs), and the University of Chicago (economics). Dr. Goodman is contributing editor for international perspectives for the *Communications of the ACM* and has served with many government, academic, professional society, and industry advisory and study groups. His research pursuits have taken him to all seven continents and about 100 countries and have included testimony before legislative bodies and ministerial-level briefings. He is currently PI on two large grants from NSF and the MacArthur Foundation. Dr. Goodman was an undergraduate at Columbia University, where he started as an aspiring English major, and obtained his Ph.D. from the California Institute of Technology (Caltech), where he worked on problems of applied mathematics and mathematical physics.

Matt Bishop is a professor of computer science at the University of California, Davis. He was a research scientist at the Research Institute of Advanced Computer Science and was on the faculty at Dartmouth College before joining the Department of Computer Science at the University of California, Davis. His main research area is the analysis of vulnerabilities in computer systems, including modeling vulnerabilities, building tools to detect them, and ameliorating or eliminating them. This work includes detecting and handling all types of malicious logic. Dr. Bishop is active in the areas of network security, the study of denial of service attacks and defenses, policy modeling, software assurance testing, and formal modeling of access control. He has also become interested in electronic voting and was one of the two PIs of the California Top-to-Bottom Review, which performed a technical review of all electronic voting systems certified in the state of California. He is active in information assurance education. His textbook, *Computer Security: Art and Science*, was published in 2002. He also teaches software engineering, machine architecture, operating systems, programming, and computer security. He received his Ph.D. in computer science in 1984 from Purdue University, where he specialized in computer security.

Mischel L. Kwon is the president of Mischel Kwon and Associates, LLC, a security consulting firm specializing in technical defensive security, security operations and information assurance. She is an IT executive with more than 29 years of experience ranging from application design and development, network architecture and deployment, information assurance policy, audit and management, technical defensive security, and large wireless system security, to building organizational and national-level computer emergency/incident response/readiness teams. Most recently, as vice president of public sector security for RSA Security, Ms. Kwon was responsible for leading RSA in assisting public sector security solutions, strategies, technologies and policy. In June 2008, she was named the director for the U.S. Computer Emergency Readiness Team (US-CERT), where she spearheaded the organization responsible for analyzing and reducing cyber threats and vulnerabilities in federal networks, disseminating cyber threat warning information, and coordinating national incident response activities. Ms. Kwon brings a unique blend of hands-on experience, academic research and training, and a seasoned understanding of how to build operational organizations from inception. Among her successes at the U.S. Department of Justice (DOJ), where she was deputy director for IT Security Staff, she built and deployed the Justice Security Operations Center to monitor and defend the DOJ network against cyber threats. In addition, she serves as an adjunct professor at George Washington University, where she also runs the George Washington University Cyber Defense Lab. Ms. Kwon holds an M.S. in computer science from Marymount University and a graduate certificate in computer security and information assurance.

Kevin R. Murphy is a consulting expert at Lamorinda Consulting, LLC and an affiliate faculty member in the Department of Psychology at Colorado State University. He was a Fulbright scholar at the University of Stockholm and is a fellow of the American Psychological Association, the Society for Industrial and Organizational Psychology, and the American Psychological Society. He is the recipient of the Society for Industrial and Organizational Psychology's 2004 Distinguished Scientific Contribution Award. He served as president of the Society for Industrial and Organizational Psychology (1997-1998) and as associate editor and then editor of the *Journal of Applied Psychology* (1991-2002), as well as editor of *Industrial and Organizational Psychology: Perspectives on Science and Practice* (2012-present). He is a member of the editorial boards of *Human Performance, Personnel Psychology, Human Resource Management Review, International Journal of Management Reviews, Journal of Industrial Psychology*, and *International Journal of Selection and Assessment*. He served as a member and chair of the Department of Defense Advisory Committee on Military Personnel Testing and has also served on four National Academy of Sciences committees, most recently the Committee to Review the Scientific Evidence on the Polygraph. He has served as an expert witness in more than 20 cases involving age, race, and sex discrimination. He is the author of more than 150 articles and book chapters and author or editor of 11 books, in areas ranging from psychometrics and statistical analysis to individual differences, performance assessment, gender, and honesty in the workplace. Dr. Murphy's main areas of research include personnel selection and placement, performance appraisal, and psychological measurement. His current work focuses on understanding the validation process. He earned his Ph.D. from Pennsylvania State University in 1979; served on the faculties of Rice University, New York University, and Colorado State University; and has had visiting appointments at the University of California, Berkeley, and the University of Limerick.

Philip M. Neches is the chairman of Foundation Ventures, LLC. He is also an independent consultant working with early-stage companies in the information technology and communications service industries on their technical, market, and business strategies as an advisor, board member, and investor. A world-renowned authority on databases, he was the founder and chief scientist of Teradata Corporation, a leading database technology vendor. He began his career as the manager for the Systems Evaluation Group at Transaction Technology, Inc. (a Citicorp subsidiary), where he led analysis of consumer banking networks, including the first large-scale deployment of automated teller machines (ATMs) in the United States. Later at Teradata, he pioneered the application of parallel processing to commercial applications. As senior vice president and chief scientist for NCR Corporation, he led both the repositioning of NCR's computer product family and the product plan for a merger with AT&T. Dr. Neches served as vice president and chief technical officer of Multimedia Products and Services Group at AT&T Corporation. He has served on the board of directors of ExpandBeyond, Inc., and on the advisory boards of EarthLink, Tacoda Systems, Luxtera, and the Technology Group of Merrill Lynch. Other prior directorships include MCC, Semitech, Dayton Public Radio, DemoGraFx, MediaMap, PeopleLink, and VendQuest. He serves on the Caltech board of trustees and sits on its technology transfer committee and chairs the student experience committee. Dr. Neches holds B.S., M.S., and Ph.D. degrees in computer science from Caltech.

Charles "Casey" O'Brien is director of the National CyberWatch Center, an NSF Advanced Technological Education-funded cybersecurity consortium headquartered at Prince George's Community College in Largo, Maryland. His major teaching and research interests include cyber exercise design and delivery, scalable and cost-effective information security laboratories, and information security curriculum development. Mr. O'Brien also teaches internationally and is a frequently invited speaker at various conferences. He has coordinated the Mid-Atlantic Collegiate Cyber Defense Competition since 2005 and is a co-founder of the National Cyber League, which was founded in 2011 with the sole purpose of providing a training ground for students to develop cybersecurity skills through combined individual and team exercises via virtual "Cyber Stadiums." Mr. O'Brien earned a B.A. in psychology from the University of St. Thomas and an M.A. in psychology from Duquesne University, and he holds various industry-recognized certifications.

Ronald P. Sanders is a senior executive advisor for Booz Allen Hamilton and the firm's first Booz Allen Hamilton fellow. Dr. Sanders supports federal and other clients in the areas of human capital, learning, and organizational transformation. He joined the firm after completing 37 years of federal service; 20 of those years were in senior executive positions. Before coming to Booz Allen, Dr. Sanders served as the U.S. intelligence community's (IC's) associate director of national intelligence and first chief human capital officer, where he played a key role in the establishment of the Office of the Director of National Intelligence (ODNI) and the integration of the IC. He also served as the Office of Personnel Management's (OPM's) first associate director for human resource policy, with responsibility for all civil service policies and programs for millions of federal employees and retirees. Among his achievements at OPM, he led the creation of the Senior Executive Service's revolutionary pay-for-performance system. Prior to his OPM appointment, Dr. Sanders served as the first chief human resources officer for the Internal Revenue Service, where he was honored for his leadership role in the service's landmark restructuring. Other executive positions include director of civilian personnel for the Department of Defense (where he received the first of his three Presidential Rank awards), founding director of the Defense Civilian Personnel Service, and deputy director of civilian personnel for the Department of the Air Force. In that latter capacity, he earned the Air Force's prestigious General Robert J. Dixon Leadership Award—the first and only civilian to be so honored. A finalist for the Service to America Career Achievement Medal, Dr. Sanders is also the recipient of the National Intelligence Distinguished Service Medal, three Presidential Rank Awards from three different agencies, two OPM Theodore Roosevelt Awards for Distinguished Public Service, and the American Society for Public Administration Award for Outstanding Career Service. He and his ODNI team also earned a coveted Harvard University Innovations in American Government award. In addition, Dr. Sanders taught and directed research centers at George Washington University and Syracuse University's Maxwell School of Citizenship and Public Affairs. He is an adjunct faculty member with the Brookings Institution Center for Public Policy Education, chairs its Executive Education Advisory Board, and sits on the board of the American Society for Training and Development. He attended MIT's Sloan School of Management Senior Executive Program and completed a congressional fellowship with the U.S. Senate Governmental Affairs Committee. A fellow of the National Academy of Public Administration, Dr. Sanders earned his doctorate in public administration from George Washington University. He also holds an M.S. degree in human resource management from the University of Utah and a B.A. degree in business management from the University of South Florida.

Appendix B

Workshop Agendas

**WORKSHOP 1: DECEMBER 12-13, 2012
NATIONAL ACADEMY OF SCIENCES
WASHINGTON, D.C.**

December 12. 2012

8:15 a.m. **Welcome**

Angela Curry, Director, National Cybersecurity Workforce Structure Strategy, Department of Homeland Security (DHS)

8:30 **Overview**

Diana Burley, George Washington University, Committee Co-Chair
Seymour Goodman, Georgia Institute of Technology, Committee Co-Chair

8:45 **Panel 1—Federal Civilian Workforce**

Steven Moxley, Senior Security Engineer, Office of the Chief Administrator, U.S. House of Representatives
Sharon James, Director, Cybersecurity Architecture and Implementation, Internal Revenue Service

Patrick Kelly, *Senior Official for Privacy, Department of Health and Human Services*

Moderator: *Mischel Kwon, Committee Member*

10:30 **Panel 2—Federal National Security and Intelligence Workforce**

Leonard T. Reinsfelder, Deputy Associate Director of Education and Training, NSA/CSS
Chris Kelsall, Branch Head, Cyberspace/Information Technology (IT) Workforce, Office of the Department of the Navy Chief Information Officer, U.S. Navy
Brian Andrzejewski, Outreach Team Lead, Futures Exploration, Defense Cyber Crime Center, Department of Defense

Moderator: *Ron Sanders, Committee Member*

12:30 p.m. **National Cybersecurity Workforce Framework**

Robin "Montana" Williams, Director, National Cybersecurity Education and Awareness Office, DHS

1:15 **Panel 3—Federal Law Enforcement Workforce**

Ed Cabrera, Assistant Special Agent in Charge (ATSAIC)-Criminal Investigative Division, U.S. Secret Service (USSS)
Trent Teyema, ATSAIC-Cyber, Washington Field Office, Federal Bureau of Investigation
Matthew Swenson, Section Chief, Computer Forensics, Cyber Crimes Center, U.S. Immigration and Customs Enforcement

Moderator: *Diana Burley, Committee Co-Chair*

2:45 **Panel 4—State and Local Government**

Cameron Kilberg, Assistant Secretary of Technology, Commonwealth of Virginia
Maribeth Luftglass, Chief Information Officer (CIO), Fairfax County Public Schools
Michael Aliperti, Senior Director of Programs, MS-ISAC (by phone)

Moderator: *Charles "Casey" O'Brien, Committee Member*

4:00 **Public Comments and Questions**

Moderator: *Diana Burley, Committee Co-Chair*

December 13, 2012

8:30 a.m. **Welcome and Housekeeping**

Diana Burley, Committee Co-Chair
Seymour Goodman, Committee Co-Chair

8:35 **Panel 5—Industry and Critical Infrastructure**

Lee Holcomb, Vice President Strategic Initiatives, Lockheed Martin Information Systems and Global Solutions
Stephanie Derdouri, Senior Advisor for Federal System Authorization and Compliance, A.I. Solutions
Byron Collie, Director, Financial Services Information Sharing and Analysis Center
Vanessa Pollock, Network Security Business Manager, Motorola
Peter Rothschild, Security Analyst and Project Manager, SRA International
Christopher Day, Chief Security Architect, Terremark
Joe Albaugh, Associate CIO and Chief Information Security Officer (CISO), U.S. Department of Transportation
Michelle Monsees, Independent Consultant

Moderator: *Philip Neches, Committee Member*

11:30 **Panel 6—Assessment and Certification: Existing and Emerging Tools**

Marc Noble, Vice Chair, Cybersecurity Certification Collaborative (C3) and International Information Systems, Security Certification Consortium, Inc., (ISC)²
Franklin Reeder, Chairman, NBISE
Rosey Greer, Rosey Greer Consulting
Alan Paller, Director of Research, SANS Institute

Moderator: *Seymour Goodman, Committee Co-Chair*

WORKSHOP 2: FEBRUARY 25-26, 2013
SAN FRANCISCO, CALIFORNIA

February 25, 2013

8:45 a.m. **Welcome**

    Robin "Montana" Williams, Director, National Cybersecurity Education and Awareness Office, DHS
    Ron Sanders, Committee Member

9:00 **Panel 1—Education, Training, and Pipeline**

    James Jones, Executive Director, Mid-Pacific Information and Communication Technologies
    Telle Whitney, Chief Executive Officer (CEO) and President, Anita Borg Institute
    Dan Manson, Professor of Computer Information Systems at California State Polytechnic University, Pomona, National Cyber League, and Cyberwatch West
    Jaishri Mehta, Cyberwatch West, Mt. San Antonio College

    Moderator: *Charles "Casey" O'Brien, Committee Member*

10:15 **Panel 2—Industry (Part 1)**

    Steve Lipner, Partner Director of Program Management, Trustworthy Computing Security, Microsoft Corporation
    John Munoz, Technical Program Manager, Google, Inc.
    Sean Mason, Director for CIRT, General Electric
    Mike McConnell, Booz Allen Hamilton

    Moderator: *Ron Sanders, Committee Member*

11:40 **Panel 3—State Government**

    Doug Robinson, Executive Director, National Association of State Chief Information Officers
    Theresa A. Masse, State CISO, Oregon
    Michele Robinson, State CISO, California
    Robert Ono, CISO, University of California, Davis

    Moderator: *Kevin Murphy, Committee Member*

2:00	**Panel 4—Industry (Part 2)**

John Stewart, Senior Vice President and Chief Security Officer, Cisco
John D. Johnson, Global Security Strategist, Deere and Company
Dickie George, Senior Advisor for Cyber Security, Applied Physics Laboratory, Johns Hopkins University

Moderator: *Mischel Kwon, Committee Member*

3:00	**Panel 5—Federal Government**

Matthew Scholl, Deputy Division Chief, Computer Security Division, National Institute of Standards and Technology
Matthew A. Parrella, Assistant United States Attorney, Chief, Computer Hacking/Intellectual Property Unit, United States Attorney's Office, Northern District of California
Brian Busony, ATSAIC-ECTF/Asset Forfeiture/Admin, U.S. Secret Service, San Francisco Field Office

Moderator: *Philip Neches, Committee Member*

4:00	**NICE Initiative Update**

Peggy Maxson, Director, National Cybersecurity Education Strategy, DHS

4:30	**Open Discussion/ Question and Answer Session**

Moderator: *Seymour Goodman, Committee Co-Chair*

February 26, 2013

8:00 a.m.	**Welcome**

Seymour Goodman, Committee Co-Chair

8:15	**(ISC)² 2013 Global Information Security Workforce Study**

Julie Peeler, Director, (ISC)² Foundation

8:45   **Panel 6—Information Technology and Cybersecurity Professional Organizations**

Jeff Frisk, Director, Certification Program, GIAC
Hord Tipton, Executive Director, (ISC)²
Eric Hibbard, CTO Security and Privacy for Hitachi Data Systems
Taylor Pellegrini, Marketing Executive, EC-Council
Eugene H. Spafford, Professor of Computer Science, Purdue University, and Chair, U.S. Public Policy Council of ACM
Terry Erdle, Executive VP for Skills Certification, CompTIA
Christopher Buse, CISO, State of Minnesota, and Member, Board of Directors, Minnesota Chapter of the Information Systems Audit and Control Association

Moderator: *Seymour Goodman, Committee Co-Chair*

WORKSHOP 3: MARCH 27, 2013
TEXAS A&M AT SAN ANTONIO

8:30 a.m.   **Welcome**

Diana Burley, Committee Co-Chair
John Dickson, Principal, Denim Group, Ltd.
Carolyn Wilson Green, Director, Center of Information Technology and Cyber Security, Texas A&M University, San Antonio
Robin "Montana" Williams, Director, National Cybersecurity Education and Awareness Office, DHS

9:00   **NICE Initiative Update**

Robin "Montana" Williams, Director, National Cybersecurity Workforce, DHS

9:30   **Panel 1—State and Local Government**

Bert Jarreau, Chief Innovation Officer, National Association of Counties
Brian Engle, CISO, Department of Information Resources, State of Texas
Greg White, Associate Professor, University of Texas, San Antonio, and Director, Center for Infrastructure Assurance and Security

Moderator: *Kevin Murphy, Committee Member*

APPENDIX B 45

10:40 **Panel 2—Cybersecurity Education, Training, and Pipeline**

Carolyn Wilson Green, Director of the Center for Information Technology and Cyber Security, Texas A&M University, San Antonio
Art Conklin, Associate Professor and Director of the Center for Information Security Research and Education, University of Houston
Troy Touchette, Chair, Computer Information Systems Department, San Antonio College
Adrian Collett, Career and Technical Education Specialist, State of Texas Education Service Center, Region 20
Scott "Skip" Runyan, Technical Advisor to the Commander, 39th Information Operations Squadron, U.S. Air Force (via teleconference)

Moderator: *Diana Burley, Committee Co-Chair*

1:00 p.m. **Panel 3—Certification and Licensing**

Roy Swift, Senior Director, Personnel Credentialing Accreditation, ANSI (by teleconference)
Lance Kinney, Executive Director, Texas Board of Professional Engineers
Jeff Pike, Senior Technical Director, GIAC

Moderator: *Seymour Goodman, Committee Co-Chair*

2:00 **Panel 4—Human Resources, Recruiting, and Talent Development**

Chris Prosise, Engineer, Pandesta
Harvinder Singh, CEO, Bestica

3:10 **Panel 5—National Security and Critical Infrastructure**

Arthur "Wally" Wachdorf, Senior Advisor for Intelligence and Cyber Operations, 24th Air Force
Guy Walsh, Technical Advisor to the Deputy Commander, U.S. Cyber Command (via teleconference)
Frank Grace, Lead Specialist, Tesoro

Moderator: *Philip Neches, Committee Member*

4:15 **Panel 6—Industry**

Rocky Destefano, Founder and CEO, VisibleRisk
Janie Gonzalez, CEO, Webhead
Sergio C. Muniz, President, CYFOR Technologies, LLC

Moderator: *Philip Neches, Committee Member*

Appendix C

Speakers and Participants at Workshops Organized by the Committee

DECEMBER 12-13, 2012, WORKSHOP SPEAKERS

Joe Albaugh, Associate Chief Information Officer and Chief Information Security Officer, U.S. Department of Transportation
Michael Aliperti, Senior Director of Programs, Multi-State Information Sharing and Analysis Center (by telephone)
Brian Andrzejewski, Outreach Team Lead, Futures Exploration, Defense Cyber Crime Center, Department of Defense
Ed Cabrera, Assistant Special Agent in Charge (ATSAIC)-Criminal Investigative Division, U.S. Secret Service (USSS)
Byron Collie, Director, Financial Services Information Sharing and Analysis Center
Angela Curry, Director, National Cybersecurity Workforce Structure Strategy, Department of Homeland Security
Christopher Day, Chief Security Architect, Terremark
Stephanie Derdouri, Senior Advisor for Federal System Authorization and Compliance, A.I. Solutions
Rosey Greer, Rosey Greer Consulting
Lee Holcomb, Vice President Strategic Initiatives, Lockheed Martin Information Systems and Global Solutions
Sharon James, Director, Cybersecurity Architecture and Implementation, Internal Revenue Service
Patrick Kelly, Senior Official for Privacy, Department of Health and Human Services

Chris Kelsall, Branch Head, Cyberspace/Information Technology (IT) Workforce, Office of the Department of the Navy Chief Information Officer, U.S. Navy
Cameron Kilberg, Assistant Secretary of Technology, Commonwealth of Virginia
Maribeth Luftglass, Chief Information Officer, Fairfax County Public Schools
Michelle Monsees, Independent Consultant
Steven Moxley, Senior Security Engineer, Office of the Chief Administrator, U.S. House of Representatives
Marc Noble, Vice Chair, Cybersecurity Certification Collaborative and International Information Systems, Security Certification Consortium, Inc.
Alan Paller, Director of Research, SANS Institute
Vanessa Pollock, Network Security Business Manager, Motorola
Franklin Reeder, Chairman, National Board of Information Security Examiners
Leonard T. Reinsfelder, Deputy Associate Director of Education and Training, NSA/CSS
Peter Rothschild, Security Analyst and Project Manager, SRA International
Matthew Swenson, Section Chief, Computer Forensics, Cyber Crimes Center, U.S. Immigration and Customs Enforcement
Trent Teyema, Assistant Special Agent in Charge-Cyber, Washington Field Office, Federal Bureau of Investigation
Robin "Montana" Williams, Director, National Cybersecurity Education and Awareness Office, Department of Homeland Security (DHS)

FEBRUARY 25-26, 2013, WORKSHOP SPEAKERS AND PARTICIPANTS

Mike Avina, Healthnet
Sarah Bohne, Senior Manager of Communications, (ISC)²
Christopher Buse, Chief Information Security Officer, State of Minnesota, and Member, Board of Directors, Minnesota Chapter of the Information Systems Audit and Control Association
Brian Busony, USSS, San Francisco Field Office
Scott Cassity, Global Information Assurance Certification
Terry Erdle, Executive Vice President for Skills Certification, CompTIA
Jeff Frisk, Director, Certification Program, GIAC
Richard M. (Dickie) George, Senior Advisor for Cyber Security, Applied Physics Laboratory, Johns Hopkins University
Eric Hibbard, Chief Technology Officer, Security and Privacy, Hitachi Data Systems

APPENDIX C

Hillary Homan, Booz Allen Hamilton
Jayson Jenkins, Booz Allen Hamilton
John D. Johnson, Global Security Strategist, Deere & Company
James Jones, Executive Director, Mid-Pacific Information and Communication Technologies
Steven LaFountain, Distinguished Academic Chair for Information Assurance and Cyber, National Security Agency
Brian LaMacchia, Microsoft Research
Steve Lipner, Partner Director of Program Management, Trustworthy Computing Security, Microsoft Corporation
Daniel Lohrmann, Chief Security Officer, State of Michigan
Dan Manson, Professor of Computer Information Systems at California State Polytechnic University, Pomona, National Cyber League, and Cyberwatch West
Sean Mason, Director, Critical Incident Response Team, General Electric
Theresa A. Masse, State Chief Information Security Officer, State of Oregon
Peggy Maxson, Director, National Cybersecurity Education Strategy, DHS
Jaishri Mehta, Cyberwatch West, Mt. San Antonio College
VADM John M. (Mike) McConnell (USN, ret.), Booz Allen Hamilton
John Munoz, Technical Program Manager, Google, Inc.
Robert Ono, Chief Information Security Officer, University of California, Davis
Randi Parker, Director, Public Advocacy, CompTIA
Matthew A. Parrella, Assistant United States Attorney, U.S. Attorney's Office for the Northern District of California
Sebron Partridge, Chief Information Security Officer, Riverside County, California
Julie Peeler, Director, (ISC)² Foundation
Taylor Pellegrini, Marketing Executive, EC-Council
James Richards, Director of IT Security, West Virginia Office of Technology
Doug Robinson, Executive Director, National Association of State Chief Information Officers
Michele Robinson, State Chief Information Security Officer, State of California
Matthew Scholl, Deputy Division Chief, Computer Security Division, National Institute of Standards and Technology
John Sjoberg
Eugene H. Spafford, Professor of Computer Science, Purdue University, and Chair, U.S. Public Policy Council of ACM
John Stewart, Senior Vice President and Chief Security Officer, Cisco
Hord Tipton, Executive Director, (ISC)²
Jodi Traversaro, Department of Human Resources, State of California

Telle Whitney, CEO and President, Anita Borg Institute
Robin "Montana" Williams, Director, National Cybersecurity Education and Awareness Office, DHS
Noel Wray, Booz Allen Hamilton

MARCH 27-28, 2013, WORKSHOP SPEAKERS AND PARTICIPANTS

Daniel Aguallo, Infinity Advisory Group
Roger Burr
John Carrera, Holmes High School, San Antonio, Texas
Brian Carron, Carron and Associates, LLC
Arthur Celestin, Southwest High School, San Antonio, Texas
Adrian Collett, Career and Technical Education Specialist, State of Texas Education Service Center, Region 20
Ron Comeau, General Dynamics
Art Conklin, Associate Professor and Director, Center for Information Security Research and Education, University of Houston
Chris Cook, Bexar Metro 9-1-1 Network District
Rocky Cortez, U.S. Air Force
Ramanamurthy Dantu, University of North Texas
Rocky Destefano, Founder and Chief Executive Officer, VisibleRisk
John Dickson, Principal, Denim Group, Ltd.
Glenn Dietrick, University of Texas, San Antonio
Brian Engle, Chief Information Security Officer, Department of Information Resources, State of Texas
Gus Gonzales III, TekFriends
Al Gonzalez, U.S. Air Force
Janie Gonzalez, Chief Executive Officer, Webhead
Matthew D. Gonzalez, University of the Incarnate Word
Mark Gottsberger, Hallmark College, San Antonio, Texas
Frank Grace, Lead Specialist, Tesoro
Carolyn Wilson Green, Director, Center for Information Technology and Cyber Security, Texas A&M University, San Antonio
Ryan Gurr, Booz Allen Hamilton
Barbara Hewitt, Texas A&M University, San Antonio
Nolen Hick, Express News, San Antonio, Texas
Mark Huson, Texas A&M University, San Antonio
Bert Jarreau, Chief Innovation Officer, National Association of Counties
Robert Kaufman, U.S. Air Force
Lance Kinney, Executive Director, Texas Board of Professional Engineers
Taryn Mandrell, Security Researcher, Alert Logic
Jason Matthews, Department of the Air Force

APPENDIX C

Chris Mock, Workforce Solutions, Alamo, Texas
Darryl Mosley, MacAulay-Brown, Inc.
Sergio C. Muniz, President, CYFOR Technologies, LLC
Lis O'Briant
Jeff Pike, Senior Technical Director, Global Information Assurance Certification
Chris Prosise, Engineer, Pandesta
Alonzo Pugh, Department of the Air Force
Rudy Ramirez, Zachary Holdings, Inc.
Scott "Skip" Runyan, Technical Advisor to the Commander, 39th Information Operations Squadron, U.S. Air Force (via teleconference)
Joe Sanchez, U.S. Air Force
Terrye Schaetzel, Georgia Tech Research Institute
Harvinder Singh, Chief Executive Officer, Bestica
Mika Spence, VisibleRisk
Roy Swift, Senior Director, Personnel Credentialing Accreditation, ANSI (via teleconference)
Troy Touchette, Chair, Computer Information Systems Department, San Antonio College
Arthur "Wally" Wachdorf, Senior Advisor for Intelligence and Cyber Operations, 24th Air Force
Guy Walsh, Technical Advisor to the Deputy Commander, U.S. Cyber Command (via teleconference)
Joules Webb, SASTEMIC
Greg White, Associate Professor, University of Texas, San Antonio, and Director, Center for Infrastructure Assurance and Security
Robin "Montana" Williams, Director, National Cybersecurity Education and Awareness Office, DHS
Vern Williams, The Patria Group
Noel Wray, Booz Allen Hamilton
Nicholas Xenos, Juniper Networks